Yours
If You
Ask

Yours If You Ask

By
Susan Polis Schutz

Designed and illustrated by
Stephen Schutz

Blue Mountain Press ™

Boulder, Colorado

The following poems have previously appeared
in Blue Mountain Arts publications:
"Fighting or disagreeing," Copyright © Continental Publications, 1976.
"I do not want," Copyright © Continental Publications, 1976.
"Last night I dreamed," Copyright © Continental Publications, 1976.
"Love is the only," Copyright © Continental Publications, 1976.
"Many relationships," Copyright © Continental Publications, 1976.
"One of the important," Copyright © Continental Publications, 1976.
"Sometimes you give," Copyright © Continental Publications, 1976.
"Though we are very close," Copyright © Continental Publications, 1976.
"We often hurt," Copyright © Continental Publications, 1976.
"We walked along the sand," Copyright © Continental Publications, 1976.
"When we get," Copyright © Continental Publications, 1976.
"You are so fair," Copyright © Continental Publications, 1977.

And from the album, "Come Into the Mountains, Dear Friend":
"I am in love," Copyright © Continental Publications, 1974, 1977.

Library of Congress Number: 78-56321
ISBN: 0-88396-028-1

Manufactured in the United States of America
First Printing: September, 1978
Second Printing: January, 1979
Third Printing: October, 1979

Blue Mountain Press INC.

P.O. Box 4549, Boulder, Colorado 80306

CONTENTS

6   This life is yours
7   Introduction
TAKE THE POWER
    TO BE HONEST WITH YOURSELF
    TO BE HONEST WITH OTHERS
    TO LOVE
11 Even though we live
13 We often hurt
14 Because I am
15 I am still the same person
17 Please be gentle
19 Am I my image
20 Ask yourself
21 I don't like phoniness
23 I must be true
24 Watching my own child
25 Some people
27 Knowing that you
28 Looking out
29 I am in love
31 One of the important
32 I had a dream
33 Before I met you
35 Sometimes you give
36 As crazy as you are
37 We walked along the sand
39 When we get
40 You are so fair
41 Love is not forever
42 There are no words
43 The sandcastles of yesterday's
    play
45 Many relationships
46 Little one

47 Don't ever hurt
48 Most people are so nice
49 I love people
51 Love is the only
52 Sometimes you make me
53 Fighting or disagreeing
55 Last night I dreamed

TAKE THE POWER
    TO CHOOSE WHAT YOU WANT TO DO
    TO CONTROL YOUR OWN LIFE
    TO BE HAPPY

59 This life is yours
60 Don't look at me
61 It is marvelous
63 I have tried
64 You want to do
65 Real Doers Do!
67 The spray of the ocean mist
68 It is so important
69 When you have done something
71 I go downtown
72 Make your life happy
75 Though I want
76 Your eyes look sick
77 If everyone would set
79 If you make
80 What happened to the sparkle
81 Closer all the time
83 I do not want
85 Though we are very close
87 If you know
90 About the Authors

This life is yours
Take the power
to choose what you want to do
and do it well
Take the power
to love what you want in life
and love it honestly
Take the power
to walk in the forest
and be a part of nature
Take the power
to control your own life
No one else can do it for you
Take the power
to make your life happy

Introduction

Yours If You Ask is my first new book in three years. A lot has happened to me during this time, and I have gone through many changes. But most important, I have learned how vital it is to do the things that make us happy and eliminate the things that don't. We are here for a very short time, and if we don't live life to its fullest now, we never will.

I believe that we all have the power within ourselves to control our own lives. Since there are so many external factors directing our lives, the process of taking control is a difficult one; but we must take the power to make our lives happy.

This life **is** yours — if you ask.

SUSAN POLIS SCHUTZ

P.S. Thank you again for listening.

Take the power

to be honest with
yourself

to be honest with
others

to love

Even though we live
far from each other
I always talk to you
in my thoughts
and see you
in my dreams
It doesn't matter
that we are not together
because our friendship
is such a strong part
of my life
And as long as I know that
you are happy where you are
I, too, am happy

We often hurt
those closest
to us.
Many times it is only
because we are
angry at ourselves,
and we scream
in furor
at someone
who understands.
I am very sorry.
I did not
mean to hurt you.

ecause I am considered successful
    you treat me
        differently
    You are afraid of me
You no longer tell me the truth
You cannot relate to me anymore
My experiences have changed and
I have grown with them
But I am the same person I have always been
It is not I who has changed
It is you and your concept
of me
that have changed

am still the same person
I was ten years ago
I'm still quiet
but confident
aggressive
but reticent
naive
but worldly
mystical
but down to earth
I'm still the same person
I was ten years ago
My hair
is as long and straight
as ever
My dress
is still jeans and turtleneck
Sandals in the summer
boots in the winter
I'm still the same person
I was ten years ago
I write
all my feelings down
on the same long yellow notebooks
and scraps of paper
I still get furious
when someone lies to me
and I get crazy
when someone is unfair
I don't like to talk much and
I still listen to music all the time
My career is an important part of my life
as are nature and my family
These are what used to make me happy
These are what make me happy still
I'm still the same person
I was ten years ago

Please be gentle
with my feelings
It will take time
because I have
been hurt
Please be gentle
with your words
It will take time
because I have heard
too many lies
Please be gentle
with your eyes
It will take time
because I have seen
too many deceitful looks
Please be gentle
with your body
It will take time
because I have felt
too many cold bodies
Please be gentle
with your love
There is a beauty
in being gentle
that only real love
can understand

Am I my image
or is my image me
Did I create my image
by things I did
or did other people
who never met me
create a way they wanted me to be
I think I know who I am
but it is
often strange
having a self
and an image
and when things get difficult
it is sometimes confusing
as to
what is real

Ask yourself
Who am I
Who are my parents
What am I
    able to do
What am I unable to do
Where am I strong
Where am I weak

Get to know yourself
What do I like to do
What do I dislike to do
What are my goals
How can I achieve them
What are my values
How can I combine my goals and values

Get to like yourself
How do I want to play
How do I not want to play
How should I act
so that I am proud of myself
How should I act
so that I am a friend to myself

 don't like
phoniness
Take off
your mask
and let me
see your face
Take off your affectation
and let me hear you talk
Take off your smile
and let me get to know you
You need the confidence
to know that you don't need
to hide
Your real self is
great

I must be true to myself
so I write only when
I am inspired
and I never write
because someone expects me to
Two and one-half years went by—
I sang
I walked in the mountains
I worked
I played
I traveled
I loved
I had many ideas
but I did not write
People yelled, "Why don't you write a book?"
I did not answer
People said, "No one will remember you."
I did not answer
People said, "Poets should continually write books."
"You must write a book!"
I did not answer
Two and one-half years went by—and one day—
a snowflake fell on a spruce tree
and it inspired me to write
Your strong profile against the sky
inspired me to write
Some pressures I was experiencing
inspired me to write
And I am now writing, writing, writing
all my feelings
all my experiences
And now I am once again
writing a book
because I am inspired and
I have been true to myself

Watching my own child
is the most amazing thing possible
and sharing this experience
   with someone I love
gives me the reason for being alive

Some people
  are so strong
that they don't need
  other people
Some people are so weak
that they need many people
I used to think that I needed a lot of people
but I was not happy that way
Then I thought that I didn't need anyone
and I was not happy that way, either
And then finally I discovered
that for me
one man to share my life with
a child
a close family and
one or two good friends
was ideal

Knowing that you are here
makes my days happier
I have always been successful
interacting with the world
but I knew that
something was missing
Now that you are here
I have discovered what was missing
It was a deep friendship

L ooking out my
        London hotel window, alone
It has started to snow
Drivers in London
        are not used to snow
so the streets are deserted
The reporters are writing
that we left nature
for two weeks
and "how do we like
big city life, the rat race,
and all our interviews?"
We love it
It really doesn't matter
where you are
as long as you are with the people you love
And the snow always
looks beautiful
no matter where you are
I think I'll take
a walk
in Hyde Park

 am in love
    with you
with your
strength and
    your warmth
always thinking
of all the good in life.
I am in love with you
with your kindness
        and truth
always looking
for all the joys in life.
I am so proud
when you look at me
so softly
and the world
  can see
     our feelings.

One of the
important aspects
of our relationship
is that neither of us
needs to be
always right, or
always strong, or
always smart, or
always first.
We have enough confidence
in ourselves and
    trust in each other
        that we can
            be our real selves
                at all times.

I had a dream last night
you were with
someone else
and kept saying
it was because
I had been so mean
I awoke suddenly
and looked at you
I wondered whether
I really had been mean to you
I think I had, but I never
intended to be
I was just acting too familiar with you
and became thoughtless
I had a dream last night
that awakened my senses

Before I met you
I was a robot
who went to work
at certain times
who played
at certain times
who laughed
at certain times
and who cried
at certain times
You awoke feelings
inside of me
that I never knew existed
As we started to get
closer and closer
you broke through the
machine of me
and discovered the
human being of me
You made my life
complete

Sometimes you give
and I take
and sometimes I give
and you take
We are learning
to go beyond
the realm of
our own selves
We are learning
to share

As crazy as you are
you're still my friend
As selfish as
    you may act sometimes
you still share my life
As weak as you pretend to be
the strength of our alliance exists
As differently as we may think
we are able to understand each other
You really know me
and I know you
That is why I always forgive you
and you always forgive me
and we will continue to
be best friends

W e walked
   along the sand
wondering why
   our relationship
is so successful in a time
when most are not
we thought about
how we respect each other
how we give each other freedom
and how we have fun together

We stopped to rest on a huge moss rock
and continued to think
how honest we are with each other
how we tell each other every feeling
we have, whether good or bad
how we never have to pretend
to each other

We ran back to the shore, holding hands
still not knowing why our
relationship is so beautiful
but very thankful that it is

When we get
bogged down
and upset with
all the everyday problems,
we don't have the
energy left
to enjoy the truly
important things—
such as our
friendship.
You have made me
realize that things
are not nearly as
devastating as they
may appear at
the moment.
You have given
me the power
to love.

You are
    so fair
so sensitive
There are
    no roles
to play with you
You are so different
from everyone else
You are free of pretension
and games
so honest
so good
By loving you
I am learning to be
a better person

Love
is not
forever
for
there is
no
forever
So to
give to a
loved one
less than
every part
of oneself
and to
treat a
loved one
with less than
complete honesty
is an
injustice
Love should be the
most beautiful and pure
emotion
one can have

T here are no words
adequate enough
to express my feelings for you
My feelings are so strong that
I can't be without you
and I want to share every second with you
They are so strong that
I want to tell you everything
and I want you to know all my thoughts
There are no words
adequate enough
to express my feelings for you
My feelings are so strong that
everything I do is affected by them
and I feel as though you are a part of my being
It is a feeling that encompasses
and goes beyond all words
and all other feelings

he sandcastles
   of yesterday's play
were still on the beach
It was early
I watched the golden sun
quietly appear above the water
I listened to the waves
as they roared on the shore
I felt the cool windy mist
as I hid under a blanket
I smelled the fragrance of the salty ocean
untouched by oil and chemicals
and I thought of you
and how I would have liked
so much, for you
to have shared this
with me

Many relationships
are fine
but I'm tired of
trying to explain
myself
I like
saying what I mean
and acting the way I feel
I like the truth
What excites
me in our relationship is that
I am able to be
my real self, truthfully
to your real self

L ittle one
you brighten up
everyone's life
that you come
in contact with
What you say
with your cute baby accent
is so fresh and cheery
Your large blue eyes are
so honest and sweet
You understand so much more
than people think
You know love
and kindness
You are love
and kindness
Little one
you brighten up
my life
all the time

 **D**on't ever hurt
        my angel
    He's too sensitive
    Don't ever lie
        to my angel
He only knows what truth is
Don't ever be harsh with my angel
He is too delicate
Don't ever be unfair to my angel
He only knows goodness
Don't ever touch my angel with maliciousness
If you do you'll have to
deal with
the devil
in me

Most people are so nice
Though they might be
different from each other
different cultures
different backgrounds
different looks
different ways of life
they have an aura of goodness
shining through their eyes
Most people are so nice
They are happy to be alive
and they are happy that
you are alive, too
They have an aura of love
shining through their eyes
and I love these people

 love
　　people
　whose eyes
　　look
　　trusting,
honest, and
innocent—
whose souls are
good,
simple, and
untouched
And I despise those
who harden these people
and force them to
change

Love is
the only true
freedom.
It lets us
cast off our
false exteriors
and be our
real
selves.

S ometimes
you make me so mad
I feel my whole body
tighten up with rage
I become completely withdrawn
and walk around like that for hours
Then I look at you
and realize that you don't even
know that you did something wrong
I also realize that I
must tell you
and I scream it out
You look so shocked
I know that any time
I tell you that you have hurt me
you are so self-blaming and
so sorry
and I immediately feel better
because what you said was unintentional
and not premeditated to hurt me
There's a big difference
I just wish I could tell you
instantly that you hurt me
rather than carrying around this burden for so long

Fighting or disagreeing is only natural. It is the working out of a solution to two different ideas that builds a lasting relationship.

Last night
I dreamed that
I was in love
with you.
This morning
I woke up
and realized that
I am in love
with you.
I am living
my dream
between
awakenings.

Take the power

to choose what you
want to do

to control your own life

to be happy

This life is yours
Take the power
to choose what you want to do
and do it well
Take the power
to love what you want in life
and love it honestly
Take the power
to walk in the forest
and be a part of nature
Take the power
to control your own life
No one else can do it for you
Take the power
to make your life happy

Don't look at me
as if I
    don't know
what I'm
    talking about
Don't talk to me
like you're trying to
explain something to a child
Don't call me names
because my goals are
similar to yours
I know this is hard for you
to understand
Your way of treating women
as secondary citizens is over
Kings do not like to share
their thrones
But we are your equal
We do know what we
are talking about
We do know everything
you are saying...and possibly more
We are going to achieve whatever
we desire
And yes,
we are truly
happy

t is marvelous
   being a woman
I love being a writer
I love being a mother
I love sharing my life with you
I, as a woman,
can be happy
as long as I am able to
control my own mind, body and life
and choose my own role to follow
rather than having society
choose a role for me
I cannot ask for more
and would not settle for less

I have tried a lot of different things
I have tried a lot of different lifestyles
And after a long journey
I gave up everything
I disliked
and went back
into the mountains
with the trees and animals
and the people I love
And once again
I started to write
and I am finally
at peace with myself
Never again will
I stray
from the things
I love

ou want
to do
one thing
You know
what is right
You know what is wrong
Yet you do another

You want to do one thing
It will make you happy
It will make you strong
Yet you do another

You want to do one thing
which will make you a new person
and give you a new life
Yet you do another

What are you so afraid of?
Why are you acting like you're dead?
Come alive again!

Real Doers DO!

Some people talk but rarely "do." This happens in all fields. Long ago someone said to me, "Man, I'm really into the Methane car," and he proceeded to talk for two straight days about how he was going to build one. But he never even started. Another person said, "I'm really into carpentry. I need to do something with my hands. It's so simple and basic. I'm going to build a dome with my own two hands. . . ." After several carpentry lessons, this person decided that building was really hard work. He never even lifted a hammer.

So many people talk and talk about what they plan on doing, but they rarely do what they say. Perhaps they are simply dreamers, or perhaps they are trying to impress the listener.

I used to always believe the "talkers," only to be disappointed later when I would ask them about their projects—and they would reply, "What projects?"

People who build houses don't talk about it. They just get some wood and start building. People who want to become actors don't just sit in coffee houses and discuss acting. They act! People who want to become writers don't talk about writing. They write! I am tired of talkers. Besides fooling the people around them, they are also fooling themselves.

Real doers do, quietly and effectively. All that talkers do is talk.

The spray of the ocean mist
the sandpiper strutting along the shore
seagulls dancing around my head
massive piles of gold seaweed
a baby rolling in the sand
a man jogging
some kids playing with a frisbee
Because I know that you are there
anytime I need you
I could sit here forever
and really enjoy this peace

t is so important
to choose your own
lifestyle
and not let others
choose it for you

When you have
   done something in life
that people like
some of them build you up
   to be a hero
You are no longer a human being
You are an object
They do not tell you the truth
You are lied to and lied about
They do not really talk to you
They say what they think you want to hear
They do not really want to get close to a hero
What they really want is to
destroy the hero that they created
tear him to pieces
and enjoy his downfall
Being a hero can be great
but it can also hurt

I go downtown to work
I'm not sure who my
friends are
and who are not
I'm not sure whom to
trust
and whom not to
I'm not sure of anything, in this world,
anymore
Back home in the mountains
I'm sure of the huge boulders
in front of the blue sky
I am sure of the tall spruce trees
outlining the rocky mountains
I am sure of the birds, and the marmots,
    and the grasshoppers
and I'm sure of
you

Make Your Life Happy

A conversation I overheard in a store between a salesperson and a customer:

Salesperson: "I don't know anyone who is happily married."

Customer: "You mean no one?"

Salesperson: "Right. Even in this store. Not one of us is happy."

Customer: "Why?"

Salesperson: "Because we didn't live in the right time. The college kids today are very smart. I wish I were young now."

Customer: "You mean you'd be promiscuous?"

Salesperson: "Well, if that's what you call it. But I can tell you, when those kids get married, they won't make the same mistakes we made. I'll tell you the truth—if I were young today, I'd never have married my husband. It's sad but true, and there's nothing I can do about it."

I have heard discussions like these from hundreds of unhappy people. Most of them, like the salesperson, are in their mid-thirties (hardly an old age). Why are they so afraid to start a new life which would make them happy? Are they afraid that they won't meet anyone else? Do they lack confidence in themselves? Do they have children and feel that a change would ruin the children? Do they feel that they do not deserve to be happy? Do they feel that because they made a mistake, they should suffer from it?

I wish that people would not be so afraid to do what they want. What they need to realize is that they have only one life, and they are living it now. If they want to be happy, they must make their own lives happy.

Though I want
people to read what I write
and I love
being known (this is what I always wanted)
and I enjoy
having an all-consuming career
I also
love privacy
and I need
solitude
and I want
to have normal relationships with people
But all this
doesn't go together
So I examined
my goals
to see
what I wanted most
Years ago, it would have been my career far ahead
but now I know that
I must be happy in
both my career and my
personal life
And I won't compromise my
personal life one bit
to help my career
because if I did
I'd be shutting out of my life
the things I like most

Your eyes look sick
They are staring at me with hate
Your mouth looks sick
and the words coming out of it are evil
Your skin looks sick
It is taut from being so tense
Your body looks sick
It is bent over from misery
Your sickness is
jealousy
and it has taken over
your entire being
so that all you can do is
hate those who are
happier than you
You'd better change fast
and start living your own life
and stop tearing others down
You'd better change fast
because your jealousy
will soon wilt more than
your body and face
It will destroy your heart
and eat your flesh
and leave nothing
but a pile
of sick
bones

If everyone would
set their own goals
and live their own lives
according to their particular desires
there would be no
jealousy in the world

If you make your own goals
If you adhere to your own values
If you choose your own kind of fun
You are living a life made by you
If other people are telling you what to do
or if you are copying other people's ways
or if you are acting out a certain lifestyle
                              to impress people
You are living for other people rather than yourself

People should not control you
You must control your own life

What happened
   to the sparkle
of sweet sixteen
   when you led the class
      in four subjects
in addition to getting voted
the most likely to succeed
Just ten years later
and fifty pounds more
you sit there
too lazy to move about
too bored to read
too bored to listen
too bored to talk
Look at this picture
It is your high school picture
It is a different person
What happened to the sparkle?

Closer all the time
Closer to myself
Closer to nature
Closer to you
Closer to love
Closer to life

I do not
want to change you
You know what
is best for you
much better than I

I do not
want you to change me
I want you to
accept me and respect me
the way I am

In this way
we can build
a strong relationship
based on reality
rather than a dream

Though we are very close
to each other,
we each have our
own lives and own goals.
We are together, always,
in our hearts,
but not necessarily
              together, always,
in all our activities—
a relationship
based on
truth and freedom.

If you know
who you are and
what you want and
why you want it
and if you have
confidence in yourself and
a strong will to obtain your desires and
a very positive attitude
you can make
your life
yours
if you ask

About The Authors

Susan began writing at age seven, and to the delight of millions of readers, she's been writing ever since. Author of five best-selling books of poetry, Susan writes without rhyme — but with all the reason in the world. Expressing her feelings on her natural surroundings, people, love and social change, Susan is endowed with a love of nature and life that she has shared with countless others.

Susan grew up in Peekskill, New York and attended Rider College in New Jersey, earning degrees in English and biology. While doing graduate work in New York City, Susan taught school in Harlem and wrote for numerous magazines and newspapers. A variety of interests and concerns kept her continually involved in new pursuits and constantly finding new outlets for her creativity.

In 1965 Susan met Stephen Schutz. Stephen, a native New Yorker, studied at the New York High School of Music and Art, where he learned the basics of drawing and calligraphy. His great love and appreciation of art became overshadowed by physics books and lab tables at M.I.T. and Princeton (where he received a Ph.D. degree in theoretical physics in 1970), but it surfaced again when he moved to Colorado for post-doctoral work. Deeply affected by the beauty of his natural surroundings, Stephen decided to give up his career in physics in order to devote all of his time to the development and perfection of his artistic techniques.

Susan and Stephen pursue paths which continually meet, diverge, and meet again. Stephen has illustrated all of Susan's books, as well as designing and illustrating books by other well known authors. He has also created a line of fine stationery featuring his gentle airbrush blends.

Susan recently released a record album containing some of her most popular poems set to music, displaying yet another manifestation of her ability and energy. She is also working on an autobiographical novel and planning the creation of a television pilot with Stephen.

A special kind of talent is required to translate feelings into poems and emotions into paintings, and Susan and Stephen have that rare gift. It is a gift that has been shared with more than 100 million people around the world. In a time of constant fluctuations in social, religious and political standards, Susan's and Stephen's expressions serve to remind us all of our inner spirit and our basic values. As a British newspaper recently commented, "her modern freestyle poems, matched by his artistry, touch the soul."

Stephen Schutz

Stephen Schutz's growing reputation as an artist comes from the innovative and recognizable style of his airbrushed illustrations. The adaptability of a scientist to techniques and experiments combined with the sensitivity of an artist to beauty are key factors for Stephen.

"Each individual printed work is an original print in its own right, rather than a reproduction of artwork. The blend of each color and the composition of every component is not finally rendered until the plate is made and the print is lithographed. All factors come into play — the paper colors and the ink mixtures — during the actual printing. I must personally supervise the first printings of all my works."

Described by American Home magazine as "a quiet, self-contained man," Stephen is an individual who has highly personal convictions. The need for independent growth, challenge and change guides his creativity. Clearly, the originality of his works is reflected in the man, himself.